Cryptocurrency Chronicles
Exploring the Digital Frontier

© Copyright 2024 by Ganiyu Sodiq - All rights reserved.

This document is geared towards providing exact and reliable information in regard to the topic and issue covered. The publication is sold with the idea that the publisher is not required to render accounting, officially permitted, or otherwise, qualified services. If advice is necessary, legal or professional, a practiced individual in the profession should be ordered.

- From a Declaration of Principles which was accepted and approved equally by a Committee of the American Bar Association and a Committee of Publishers and Associations.

In no way is it legal to reproduce, duplicate, or transmit any part of this document in either electronic means or in printed format. Recording of this publication is strictly prohibited and any storage of this document is not allowed unless with written permission from the publisher. All rights reserved.

The information provided herein is stated to be truthful and consistent, in that any liability, in terms of inattention or otherwise, by any usage or abuse of any policies, processes, or directions contained within is the solitary and utter responsibility of the recipient reader. Under no circumstances will any legal responsibility or blame be held against the publisher for any reparation, damages, or monetary loss due to the information herein, either directly or indirectly.

Respective authors own all copyrights not held by the publisher.

The information herein is offered for informational purposes solely and is universal as so. The presentation of the information is without contract or any type of guarantee assurance.

The trademarks that are used are without any consent, and the publication of the trademark is without permission or backing by the trademark owner. All trademarks and brands within this book are for clarifying purposes only and are the owned by the owners themselves, not affiliated with this document.

Table of Contents

Chapter One 3
- Prelude to the Digital Revolution 3
- Bitcoin: A Decade of Disruption 6
- Ethereum and the Smart Contract Revolution 8

Chapter Two 11
- Altcoins and the Diversification Dilemma 11
- The Promise of Decentralized Finance (DeFi) 13
- Navigating Regulatory Waters 15

Chapter Three 18
- Cryptocurrency Security: Safeguarding Your Digital Assets 18
- The Role of Institutions: Wall Street Meets Crypto 20
- Cryptocurrency and Social Impact 22

Chapter Four 24
- The Future of Money: Emerging Trends and Innovations 24
- Beyond Currency: Blockchain Applications Across Industries 26
- The Rise of Decentralized Autonomous Organizations (DAOs) 28

Chapter Five 31
- The Intersection of AI and Blockchain: Exploring Synergies 31
- Cryptocurrency in Emerging Markets: Opportunities and Challenges 33
- Sustainable Cryptocurrency: Environmental Solutions and Green Initiatives 35

Chapter Six 38

    Privacy Coins and the Quest for Financial Privacy 38
    Decentralized Identity and Self-Sovereign Identity (SSI) 40
    Exploring Cross-Chain Interoperability 42

Chapter Seven 45

    Quantum Computing and the Future of Cryptography 45
    Social Impact of Cryptocurrency Philanthropy and Community Building 47
    The Evolution of Central Bank Digital Currencies (CBDCs) 49

Chapter Eight 52

    Regenerative Finance: Blockchain Solutions for Environmental Conservation 52
    The Future of Work: Decentralized Autonomous Workforces (DAWs) 54
    Web3: Building the Decentralized Internet of the Future 56

Chapter Nine 58

    The Metaverse Economy: Virtual Assets and Digital Realities ... 58
    Quantum Blockchain: Securing the Future of Cryptocurrency .. 60
    Bridging the Gap: Empowering Underserved Communities with Blockchain 62

Chapter Ten 65

    Revolutionizing Healthcare with Blockchain Technology 65
    AI-Powered Cryptocurrency Trading and Risk Management 67

Conclusion 70

Chapter One

Prelude to the Digital Revolution

In the annals of human civilization, the concept of money has been a driving force, shaping economies, societies, and even individual destinies. From the earliest forms of barter to the intricate financial systems of today, the evolution of money is a testament to humanity's ingenuity and adaptability. It's a journey marked by innovation, necessity, and the constant quest for efficiency.

Money, in its simplest form, emerged as a medium of exchange, facilitating trade and commerce between individuals and communities. In ancient civilizations, commodities such as grain, livestock, and precious metals served as early forms of currency, their value determined by their utility and scarcity. These primitive systems laid the groundwork for more sophisticated monetary systems to come.

As societies grew and trade networks expanded, the need for standardized units of exchange became apparent. Thus, the concept of coinage was born, with governments and ruling authorities minting metal coins to serve as official currency. These coins, bearing the insignias of kings and emperors, not only facilitated trade but also symbolized power and authority.

The advent of paper money in China during the Tang Dynasty marked a significant milestone in the evolution of money. Initially, paper currency was backed by precious metals stored in government treasuries, providing a more convenient and portable alternative to cumbersome metal coins. Over time, paper money became widely adopted across civilizations, paving the way for modern fiat currencies.

The modern monetary system, characterized by fiat currencies issued and regulated by central banks, emerged in the wake of the Industrial Revolution. With the rise of complex financial institutions and global trade networks, the need for a stable and universally accepted medium of exchange became paramount. Fiat currencies, backed by the trust and authority of governments, became the cornerstone of the modern economy.

However, the centralized nature of traditional financial systems has long been a point of contention. Issues such as inflation, currency manipulation, and economic inequality have fueled discontent and sparked calls for alternative monetary systems. Enter cryptocurrency – a revolutionary new form of digital currency that seeks to disrupt the traditional financial landscape.

The story of cryptocurrency begins with a pseudonymous figure known as Satoshi Nakamoto. In 2008, Nakamoto published a seminal whitepaper titled "Bitcoin: A Peer-to-Peer Electronic Cash System," outlining the principles of a decentralized digital currency. The identity of Satoshi Nakamoto remains shrouded in mystery, with speculation and theories abound, but the impact of their creation is undeniable.

At the heart of cryptocurrency lies blockchain technology – a decentralized ledger system that records all transactions across a network of computers. Unlike traditional financial systems, which rely on centralized authorities to verify and validate transactions, blockchain operates on a peer-to-peer network, with transactions being verified by network participants known as miners.

Blockchain technology ensures transparency, security, and immutability, making it the backbone of cryptocurrency. Each transaction is cryptographically secured and stored in a block, which is then linked to the preceding block, forming a chain of blocks – hence the name blockchain. This distributed ledger system eliminates the need for intermediaries, such as banks or clearinghouses, reducing transaction costs and increasing efficiency.

The decentralized nature of blockchain technology also enhances security, making it resistant to hacking and tampering. Each transaction is verified by multiple nodes on the network, ensuring consensus and preventing fraudulent activity. This trustless system allows users to transact directly with one another, without the need for third-party oversight or approval.

In summary, the evolution of money has been a journey marked by innovation, adaptation, and the relentless pursuit of progress. From the barter systems of ancient civilizations to the decentralized digital currencies of today, the concept of money continues to evolve, driven by advances in technology and shifts in societal norms. Cryptocurrency, with its promise of decentralization and financial sovereignty, represents the latest chapter in this ongoing saga – a testament to humanity's boundless creativity and resilience.

Bitcoin: A Decade of Disruption

In the ever-evolving landscape of digital finance, few phenomena have captured the public imagination quite like Bitcoin. Born out of the ashes of the 2008 financial crisis and introduced to the world in a whitepaper by the enigmatic Satoshi Nakamoto, Bitcoin quickly gained traction among a niche community of tech enthusiasts and libertarians. Yet, its journey from obscurity to mainstream sensation is a testament to the transformative power of disruptive technologies.

Bitcoin's rise to prominence was anything but conventional. In its infancy, the cryptocurrency faced skepticism and derision from traditional financial institutions and regulatory bodies. Critics dismissed it as a passing fad, a speculative bubble destined to burst. However, as its decentralized nature and finite supply became apparent, Bitcoin began to attract a dedicated following of believers who saw it as a hedge against the uncertainties of fiat currency.

As Bitcoin's popularity grew, so too did its market dynamics and price volatility. The cryptocurrency's price swings became the stuff of legend, with dramatic fluctuations occurring within hours, if not minutes. Volatility, fueled by factors such as market sentiment, regulatory announcements, and macroeconomic trends, became both a blessing and a curse for investors and traders alike.

Despite its volatility, Bitcoin has emerged as a store of value for many investors, earning comparisons to traditional safe-haven assets like gold. Proponents argue that Bitcoin's fixed supply – capped at 21 million coins – makes it resistant to inflation and currency devaluation. Its decentralized nature, secured by the underlying blockchain technology, offers a level of transparency and security unmatched by traditional financial instruments.

However, the debate rages on: is Bitcoin a digital gold or a speculative asset? Critics point to its price volatility and lack of intrinsic value as evidence of its speculative nature. They argue that its value is purely speculative, driven by hype and market sentiment rather than underlying fundamentals. Yet, proponents remain steadfast in their belief that Bitcoin represents a paradigm shift in finance – a digital asset with the potential to reshape the global economy.

For many investors, Bitcoin's appeal lies in its potential for outsized returns. The cryptocurrency's meteoric rise from mere cents to thousands of dollars per coin has minted millionaires and billionaires overnight. Yet, with great reward comes great risk, and Bitcoin's rollercoaster price movements have left many investors reeling from losses.

Despite the uncertainties and risks associated with Bitcoin, its journey from obscurity to mainstream sensation is a testament to the power of disruptive technologies to challenge the status quo. Whether it ultimately proves to be a digital gold or a speculative asset remains to be seen. Yet, one thing is certain: Bitcoin has irrevocably altered the financial landscape, sparking a global conversation about the future of money and the role of decentralized technologies in shaping it.

Ethereum and the Smart Contract Revolution

In the realm of cryptocurrency, Ethereum stands as a beacon of innovation, offering a platform for decentralized applications (DApps) and smart contracts. At its helm is Vitalik Buterin, a visionary programmer whose groundbreaking ideas have reshaped the landscape of blockchain technology.

Vitalik Buterin's journey began in 2013 when he conceptualized Ethereum as a decentralized platform that could go beyond Bitcoin's capabilities. Drawing inspiration from Bitcoin's blockchain, Buterin sought to create a more versatile platform that could support a wide range of applications beyond simple peer-to-peer transactions.

In 2014, Buterin published the Ethereum whitepaper, outlining his vision for a decentralized platform with Turing-complete scripting language, enabling developers to build complex smart contracts and DApps. This marked the birth of the Ethereum network – a groundbreaking project that would revolutionize the way we think about blockchain technology.

At the heart of Ethereum's innovation lies smart contracts – self-executing contracts with the terms of the agreement directly written into code. These contracts automatically enforce the terms and conditions of an agreement, eliminating the need for intermediaries and reducing the risk of fraud or manipulation.

Smart contracts have the potential to redefine trust and automation in a wide range of industries. From financial services to supply chain management, smart contracts offer a more efficient and transparent way to conduct business. They enable parties to enter into agreements without relying on third-party intermediaries, streamlining processes and reducing costs.

Ethereum's impact extends far beyond smart contracts, however. Its introduction of decentralized finance (DeFi) has unlocked new possibilities for financial innovation and inclusion. DeFi encompasses a range of financial services and applications built on decentralized networks, including lending, borrowing, trading, and asset management.

One of the most significant developments in the DeFi space is the creation of decentralized exchanges (DEXs), which enable users to trade cryptocurrencies directly with one another without the need for a central authority. These platforms offer greater liquidity, lower fees, and enhanced privacy compared to traditional centralized exchanges.

Ethereum has also catalyzed the emergence of the token economy – a digital ecosystem where assets are represented by tokens on the blockchain. These tokens can represent anything of value, from cryptocurrencies to real-world assets like real estate or art. Ethereum's ERC-20 standard, which defines a set of rules for creating tokens on its blockchain, has become the foundation for a thriving ecosystem of digital assets.

The token economy has paved the way for innovative crowdfunding mechanisms such as initial coin offerings (ICOs) and tokenized securities. These fundraising methods enable startups to raise capital directly from a global audience of investors, bypassing traditional venture capital channels.

In summary, Vitalik Buterin's vision for Ethereum has ushered in a new era of decentralized innovation. From smart contracts to DeFi and the token economy, Ethereum has fundamentally changed the way we think about technology and finance. As the Ethereum network continues to evolve and mature, its impact on the world is likely to grow exponentially, shaping the future of decentralized technology for years to come.

Chapter Two

Altcoins and the Diversification Dilemma

In the expansive universe of cryptocurrencies, Bitcoin and Ethereum may be the household names, but they are far from the only players in the game. Enter altcoins – alternative cryptocurrencies that offer unique features, use cases, and investment opportunities. Navigating this diverse landscape requires a keen understanding of the various altcoins available and the strategies for evaluating their potential.

Ripple, Litecoin, and Stellar are among the most prominent altcoins, each with its own set of features and objectives. Ripple, known for its digital payment protocol, aims to facilitate fast, low-cost cross-border transactions for financial institutions. Its native cryptocurrency, XRP, serves as a bridge currency, facilitating the exchange of value between different fiat currencies.

Litecoin, often referred to as the silver to Bitcoin's gold, is a peer-to-peer cryptocurrency that boasts faster transaction times and lower fees compared to its predecessor. Created by Charlie Lee in 2011, Litecoin aims to be a practical digital currency for everyday transactions, offering a more efficient and scalable alternative to Bitcoin.

Stellar, founded by Jed McCaleb in 2014, is another altcoin with a focus on facilitating cross-border payments and remittances. Stellar's network enables fast and affordable transactions, making it particularly well-suited for micropayments and financial inclusion initiatives. Its native cryptocurrency, Lumens (XLM), serves as the fuel that powers transactions on the Stellar network.

Investing in altcoins requires careful consideration and due diligence. With thousands of altcoins available in the market, it's essential to develop a discerning eye for identifying projects with genuine potential. One strategy for evaluating altcoin projects is to assess the team behind the project – their experience, track record, and vision for the future.

Another crucial factor to consider is the technology underlying the altcoin. Does it offer any innovative features or improvements over existing cryptocurrencies? Does it address a real-world problem or market demand? Conducting thorough research into the technology and development roadmap of an altcoin can provide valuable insights into its long-term viability.

Community support and adoption are also critical indicators of an altcoin's potential success. Projects with active and engaged communities are more likely to attract users, developers, and investors, driving demand for the cryptocurrency and increasing its value over time. Social media channels, forums, and developer communities can provide valuable insights into the level of support and enthusiasm surrounding an altcoin.

Furthermore, evaluating the market dynamics and ecosystem surrounding an altcoin can help assess its investment potential. Factors such as liquidity, trading volume, and exchange support can impact the liquidity and accessibility of an altcoin, influencing its price stability and investment appeal.

Diversification is another key strategy for investing in altcoins. By spreading your investment across a diverse portfolio of altcoins, you can mitigate risk and maximize potential returns. However, it's essential to strike a balance between risk and reward, carefully considering factors such as market trends, volatility, and portfolio allocation.

Altcoins offer a diverse array of investment opportunities beyond Bitcoin and Ethereum. By exploring unique use cases, evaluating altcoin projects, and adopting sound investment strategies, investors can navigate the altcoin landscape with confidence and capitalize on the potential of this dynamic and rapidly evolving market.

The Promise of Decentralized Finance (DeFi)

Decentralized Finance, or DeFi, has emerged as one of the most exciting and rapidly growing sectors within the cryptocurrency space. Unlike traditional finance, which relies on centralized institutions such as banks and exchanges, DeFi aims to democratize access to financial services by leveraging blockchain technology to create open and permissionless systems.

At its core, DeFi seeks to replicate and expand upon traditional financial services in a decentralized manner. This includes borrowing and lending, trading, asset management, and more, all without the need for intermediaries. By eliminating middlemen and reducing barriers to entry, DeFi has the potential to revolutionize the way we think about finance.

One of the key concepts in DeFi is yield farming, which involves providing liquidity to decentralized exchanges (DEXs) or lending platforms in exchange for rewards. Liquidity providers earn fees generated by trading activity on these platforms, as well as additional incentives such as governance tokens or yield farming rewards. Yield farming has become increasingly popular among DeFi enthusiasts, offering the potential for passive income and high returns.

Liquidity pools are essential components of decentralized exchanges and lending platforms in the DeFi ecosystem. These pools consist of funds provided by users, which are used to facilitate trades or provide loans to borrowers. By pooling their funds together, users can access deeper liquidity and reduce slippage when trading cryptocurrencies or borrowing assets.

Automated Market Makers (AMMs) play a crucial role in decentralized exchanges by enabling liquidity provision and price discovery without the need for traditional order books. Instead of relying on buyers and sellers to match orders, AMMs use algorithms to determine asset prices based on supply and demand within liquidity pools. This automated process ensures continuous liquidity and enables seamless trading for users.

While DeFi offers exciting opportunities for innovation and financial inclusion, it also presents challenges and risks that must be carefully considered. One of the primary challenges facing the DeFi ecosystem is scalability. As the popularity of DeFi applications grows, so too does the strain on blockchain networks, leading to congestion and high transaction fees.

Security is another major concern in the DeFi space, as smart contract vulnerabilities and exploits have led to significant losses for users and investors. Despite efforts to audit and secure DeFi protocols, the risk of bugs or hacks remains a persistent threat. Additionally, regulatory uncertainty looms over the DeFi ecosystem, as policymakers grapple with how to regulate these decentralized and borderless financial services.

Despite these challenges, the DeFi ecosystem continues to grow and evolve, fueled by a vibrant community of developers, investors, and enthusiasts. Innovations such as flash loans, decentralized derivatives, and synthetic assets are pushing the boundaries of what is possible in decentralized finance, opening up new opportunities for financial experimentation and creativity.

DeFi represents a paradigm shift in the way we think about finance, offering unprecedented access, transparency, and innovation in the world of decentralized finance. By understanding the fundamentals of DeFi, exploring concepts like yield farming and liquidity pools, and acknowledging the challenges and opportunities that lie ahead, investors can navigate this exciting and rapidly evolving ecosystem with confidence.

Navigating Regulatory Waters

Navigating the regulatory landscape of the cryptocurrency industry is akin to traversing a complex maze, with regulations varying from one jurisdiction to another. The global patchwork of laws and guidelines governing cryptocurrencies reflects the diverse attitudes and approaches of governments and regulatory bodies worldwide.

In some countries, cryptocurrencies are embraced as a tool for innovation and economic growth, while in others, they are met with skepticism and stringent regulations. The regulatory environment for cryptocurrencies can range from permissive and forward-thinking to restrictive and hostile, creating uncertainty for businesses and investors operating in the space.

Cryptocurrency exchanges and projects face a myriad of regulatory challenges as they seek to comply with often ambiguous and evolving regulations. Compliance requirements can include anti-money laundering (AML) and know your customer (KYC) procedures, licensing and registration requirements, tax obligations, and more. Failure to adhere to these regulations can result in legal penalties, fines, or even the closure of businesses.

One of the biggest challenges facing cryptocurrency exchanges is obtaining banking relationships and access to financial services. Many banks are reluctant to work with cryptocurrency-related businesses due to regulatory concerns, compliance risks, and reputational issues. This lack of banking support can hinder the growth and development of the cryptocurrency industry, making it difficult for exchanges to operate efficiently and serve their customers.

The future of cryptocurrency regulation remains uncertain, as policymakers grapple with how to balance innovation and stability in this rapidly evolving space. While some countries have taken proactive steps to regulate cryptocurrencies and provide clarity for businesses and investors, others have adopted a more cautious approach, opting to monitor developments and assess risks before taking action.

Regulation of cryptocurrencies is likely to continue to evolve as governments and regulatory bodies gain a better understanding of the technology and its implications. International cooperation and coordination will be crucial in addressing cross-border challenges and ensuring consistency and coherence in regulatory frameworks.

Ultimately, the goal of cryptocurrency regulation should be to protect investors and consumers while fostering innovation and competition in the digital economy. Achieving this balance will require collaboration between governments, regulators, industry stakeholders, and the broader community to develop clear, effective, and enforceable regulations that support the growth and maturation of the cryptocurrency industry.

As the cryptocurrency industry continues to mature, regulatory compliance will become increasingly important for businesses and investors alike. By staying informed about the regulatory landscape, understanding compliance requirements, and engaging with regulators and policymakers, stakeholders can navigate the complex regulatory environment and contribute to the responsible growth and development of the cryptocurrency ecosystem.

Chapter Three

Cryptocurrency Security: Safeguarding Your Digital Assets

When it comes to protecting your cryptocurrency assets, security is paramount. Wallet security best practices are essential for safeguarding your funds against theft, hacks, and other security threats. Cold storage, hardware wallets, and multisig are among the most effective strategies for keeping your cryptocurrency safe from unauthorized access.

Cold storage is a method of storing cryptocurrency offline, away from internet-connected devices, to minimize the risk of hacking or theft. Cold storage solutions include hardware wallets, paper wallets, and offline storage devices. By keeping your private keys offline, you can significantly reduce the risk of unauthorized access to your funds.

Hardware wallets are specialized devices designed specifically for storing cryptocurrency securely. These devices store your private keys offline and require physical access and authentication to access your funds. Hardware wallets are considered one of the most secure options for storing cryptocurrency, as they are immune to online hacking attempts and malware attacks.

Multisig, short for multi-signature, is a security feature that requires multiple private keys to authorize a cryptocurrency transaction. With multisig, you can distribute the responsibility for controlling your funds among multiple parties, reducing the risk of a single point of failure. This added layer of security makes it more difficult for hackers to access your funds without authorization.

Protecting against hacks, scams, and phishing attempts is essential for maintaining the security of your cryptocurrency holdings. Hackers and scammers often use phishing emails, fake websites, and malware to trick users into revealing their private keys or other sensitive information. By staying vigilant and following security best practices, you can reduce the risk of falling victim to these attacks.

One of the most important security precautions you can take is to use strong, unique passwords for your cryptocurrency accounts and wallets. Avoid using the same password for multiple accounts, and consider using a password manager to generate and store complex passwords securely. Additionally, be wary of unsolicited communications or requests for sensitive information, especially from unknown or untrusted sources.

Insurance and custodial solutions offer an additional layer of protection for cryptocurrency investors and traders. Some cryptocurrency exchanges and custodians offer insurance coverage for customer funds, protecting against losses due to hacking, theft, or other security breaches. While insurance can provide peace of mind, it's essential to carefully review the terms and coverage limits of any insurance policy before entrusting your funds to a third party.

Custodial solutions, such as cryptocurrency exchanges and wallet providers, offer convenience and accessibility for users who prefer to delegate the responsibility of managing their funds. However, custodial solutions also come with inherent risks, as users must trust the custodian to safeguard their funds securely. When choosing a custodial solution, be sure to research the provider's security practices and reputation to ensure the safety of your cryptocurrency holdings.

Wallet security best practices are essential for protecting your cryptocurrency assets from theft, hacks, and other security threats. By using cold storage, hardware wallets, and multisig, you can minimize the risk of unauthorized access to your funds. Additionally, staying vigilant against hacks, scams, and phishing attempts, and considering insurance and custodial solutions can help mitigate risk and ensure the security of your cryptocurrency holdings.

The Role of Institutions: Wall Street Meets Crypto

Institutional adoption of cryptocurrency marks a significant shift in the perception and acceptance of digital assets within traditional financial circles. Once viewed with skepticism and caution, cryptocurrencies have now captured the attention of institutional investors, leading to what some have dubbed "institutional FOMO" – fear of missing out on the potential gains offered by this emerging asset class.

Bitcoin exchange-traded funds (ETFs), futures contracts, and derivatives have played a pivotal role in driving institutional adoption of cryptocurrency. These financial products provide institutional investors with regulated and familiar avenues for gaining exposure to digital assets, mitigating some of the perceived risks associated with direct ownership of cryptocurrencies.

Bitcoin ETFs, in particular, have garnered significant interest from institutional investors seeking exposure to the world's largest cryptocurrency. These investment vehicles allow investors to buy and sell shares in a fund that holds Bitcoin, providing a convenient and regulated way to invest in the digital asset. While the U.S. Securities and Exchange Commission (SEC) has yet to approve a Bitcoin ETF, several countries, including Canada and Germany, have already launched their own Bitcoin ETFs, paving the way for greater institutional participation in the cryptocurrency market.

Futures contracts and derivatives offer another avenue for institutional investors to gain exposure to cryptocurrencies while managing risk. Futures contracts allow investors to speculate on the future price of Bitcoin, providing opportunities for hedging and risk management. Derivatives such as options and swaps also enable investors to customize their exposure to cryptocurrencies, offering flexibility and liquidity in the market.

The growing participation of institutional investors in the cryptocurrency market has had a profound impact on market dynamics, influencing liquidity, volatility, and price discovery. Institutional investors, with their deep pockets and risk management strategies, have brought increased liquidity to the market, reducing spreads and improving price efficiency. This increased liquidity has also helped to dampen volatility in the cryptocurrency market, making it more attractive to institutional investors and mainstream adoption.

However, institutional involvement in the cryptocurrency market has not been without its challenges. Regulatory uncertainty, custody concerns, and market manipulation are among the key issues that have hindered greater institutional participation in the cryptocurrency market. Regulatory clarity and robust infrastructure for custody and settlement are essential for attracting institutional investors and fostering greater confidence in the market.

Despite these challenges, the growing institutional adoption of cryptocurrency represents a significant milestone in the maturation of the industry. As institutional investors continue to allocate capital to digital assets, the cryptocurrency market is likely to become more integrated with traditional financial markets, leading to greater liquidity, stability, and mainstream acceptance.

Institutional adoption of cryptocurrency is transforming the landscape of the financial industry, with Bitcoin ETFs, futures, and derivatives playing a central role in driving institutional participation. While challenges remain, the growing interest from institutional investors bodes well for the future of the cryptocurrency market, paving the way for greater liquidity, stability, and adoption in the years to come.

Cryptocurrency and Social Impact

Cryptocurrency has the potential to revolutionize financial inclusion by providing access to banking services for the unbanked and underbanked populations worldwide. Traditional banking systems often exclude large segments of the population due to factors such as geographical location, lack of documentation, or high fees. Cryptocurrency offers a decentralized alternative that can be accessed with just a smartphone and an internet connection, enabling individuals to participate in the global economy without the need for traditional banking services.

One of the most significant benefits of cryptocurrency for financial inclusion is its ability to facilitate remittances and cross-border payments at a fraction of the cost and time of traditional financial systems. Migrants and expatriates often rely on costly remittance services to send money back to their home countries, with fees averaging around 7% of the transaction amount. Cryptocurrency eliminates the need for intermediaries, allowing individuals to send funds directly to recipients across borders quickly and affordably.

However, the environmental impact of cryptocurrency mining has raised concerns about its sustainability and carbon footprint. Cryptocurrency mining, the process by which new coins are created and transactions are verified on the blockchain, requires significant amounts of energy, often sourced from fossil fuels. As the demand for cryptocurrency grows, so too does the energy consumption associated with mining, leading to concerns about its environmental impact and contribution to climate change.

Addressing environmental concerns associated with cryptocurrency mining will require innovative solutions and a shift towards more sustainable mining practices. Some projects are exploring alternative consensus mechanisms that require less energy than traditional proof-of-work mining, such as proof-of-stake or proof-of-authority. Additionally, efforts to increase transparency and accountability in the mining industry, such as the use of renewable energy sources and carbon offsetting initiatives, can help mitigate the environmental impact of cryptocurrency mining.

Cryptocurrency has the potential to promote financial inclusion by providing access to banking services for the unbanked and underbanked populations. Its ability to facilitate remittances and cross-border payments at lower costs and faster speeds than traditional financial systems makes it a powerful tool for individuals and communities worldwide. However, addressing environmental concerns associated with cryptocurrency mining will be essential to ensuring its long-term sustainability and minimizing its impact on the environment.

Chapter Four

The Future of Money: Emerging Trends and Innovations

The intersection of the metaverse and non-fungible tokens (NFTs) represents a groundbreaking convergence of digital art and cryptocurrency. The metaverse, a virtual reality space where users can interact with each other and digital environments, provides a new canvas for artists to showcase their work and for collectors to acquire unique digital assets. NFTs, which are digital tokens representing ownership of unique items or assets, have become a popular medium for buying, selling, and trading digital art within the metaverse.

Central bank digital currencies (CBDCs) are digital versions of fiat currencies issued by central banks. These digital currencies aim to modernize the financial system, enhance payment efficiency, and foster financial inclusion. Countries around the world are exploring the feasibility of launching CBDCs, with some already piloting or implementing digital currency projects. The race toward digital sovereignty is driven by the recognition of the transformative potential of CBDCs to reshape the global financial landscape.

Scalability solutions and layer 2 protocols are essential for overcoming the limitations of blockchain technology, such as slow transaction speeds and high fees. These solutions aim to increase the throughput and efficiency of blockchain networks, enabling them to process a higher volume of transactions at lower costs. Layer 2 protocols, such as sidechains and state channels, build on top of existing blockchains to provide additional scalability and functionality without compromising security or decentralization.

In the metaverse, NFTs are revolutionizing the way we create, own, and exchange digital art and assets. Artists can tokenize their creations as NFTs, allowing them to retain ownership and monetize their work in new and innovative ways. Collectors can purchase NFTs as unique digital assets, providing a means of supporting their favorite artists and owning exclusive digital collectibles. The metaverse serves as a virtual gallery where NFTs can be displayed and traded, creating a vibrant ecosystem for digital art and culture.

CBDCs represent a significant evolution in the concept of money, offering central banks greater control and oversight of the financial system. By digitizing fiat currencies, CBDCs can streamline payment processes, reduce transaction costs, and enhance financial inclusion. CBDCs also provide central banks with valuable data insights into the flow of money within the economy, enabling more informed monetary policy decisions. However, the implementation of CBDCs raises questions about privacy, security, and the role of central banks in the digital age.

Scalability solutions and layer 2 protocols are essential for unlocking the full potential of blockchain technology. By increasing transaction throughput and reducing fees, these solutions enable blockchain networks to support a wide range of applications and use cases, from decentralized finance (DeFi) to non-fungible tokens (NFTs). Layer 2 protocols, in particular, offer a scalable and flexible approach to building scalable blockchain applications, allowing developers to experiment with new ideas and innovations without being limited by the constraints of the underlying blockchain.

The metaverse and NFTs are transforming the digital art landscape, providing artists and collectors with new opportunities for creativity, ownership, and interaction. CBDCs are reshaping the global financial system, offering central banks greater control and oversight of monetary policy. Scalability solutions and layer 2 protocols are addressing the scalability challenges of blockchain technology, paving the way for mass adoption and mainstream use. Together, these developments represent the next frontier in the evolution of cryptocurrency and blockchain technology.

Beyond Currency: Blockchain Applications Across Industries

Supply chain management has long been plagued by challenges such as inefficiency, fraud, and lack of transparency. Blockchain technology offers a solution by providing a secure and immutable ledger for tracking and verifying transactions across the supply chain. By recording every step of the production and distribution process on the blockchain, companies can enhance transparency and traceability, reducing the risk of counterfeit goods, improving efficiency, and building trust with consumers.

In the healthcare industry, protecting sensitive patient data and ensuring the integrity of medical records are top priorities. Blockchain technology offers a decentralized and secure solution for managing healthcare data, providing patients with greater control over their medical information and enabling healthcare providers to securely share data across systems. By encrypting patient data and recording transactions on the blockchain, healthcare organizations can enhance privacy, security, and interoperability, ultimately improving patient outcomes and streamlining administrative processes.

Identity management is another area where blockchain technology shows promise. Traditional identity systems are often fragmented and prone to data breaches, leading to identity theft and fraud. Blockchain-based identity solutions offer a decentralized and tamper-proof alternative, allowing individuals to control their digital identities and securely share personal information with trusted parties. By leveraging cryptographic techniques and distributed ledger technology, blockchain identity solutions enable secure and seamless identity verification, reducing the risk of fraud and improving access to services.

Beyond supply chain management, healthcare, and identity management, blockchain technology is finding applications in a wide range of industries and use cases. In the real estate sector, blockchain-based platforms are revolutionizing property transactions by streamlining processes, reducing paperwork, and improving transparency. Smart contracts, which are self-executing contracts with the terms of the agreement directly written into code, enable automated and secure real estate transactions, eliminating the need for intermediaries and reducing the risk of disputes.

In the gaming industry, blockchain technology is transforming the way games are developed, distributed, and monetized. Blockchain-based gaming platforms offer players true ownership of in-game assets, enabling them to buy, sell, and trade digital items with other players. NFTs, or non-fungible tokens, allow developers to create unique and rare digital assets that can be bought, sold, and collected by players, creating new revenue streams and opportunities for game developers and players alike.

These are just a few examples of the emerging use cases for blockchain technology across various industries. As the technology continues to evolve and mature, we can expect to see even more innovative applications and solutions leveraging the power of blockchain to solve real-world problems, drive efficiencies, and create new opportunities for businesses and consumers alike. Whether it's supply chain management, healthcare, identity management, real estate, gaming, or beyond, blockchain technology is poised to revolutionize the way we live, work, and interact in the digital age.

The Rise of Decentralized Autonomous Organizations (DAOs)

Decentralized Autonomous Organizations (DAOs) represent a new paradigm in organizational governance, decision-making, and tokenomics. Unlike traditional centralized organizations, DAOs are governed by smart contracts and consensus mechanisms, allowing participants to collectively make decisions and manage resources without the need for intermediaries or central authorities. DAOs operate on blockchain networks, enabling transparency, security, and decentralization in the management of digital assets and resources.

DAOs have gained traction across various industries, from finance and governance to art and entertainment. Examples of successful DAOs include decentralized finance (DeFi) protocols such as MakerDAO and Compound, which enable users to borrow, lend, and earn interest on cryptocurrencies using smart contracts and automated systems. Other notable examples include decentralized social media platforms like Steemit and decentralized autonomous art organizations like Flamingo DAO, which enable artists and creators to tokenize and monetize their work directly on the blockchain.

However, DAOs are not without controversy and challenges. The most notable example is The DAO, a decentralized investment fund built on the Ethereum blockchain that was hacked in 2016, resulting in the loss of millions of dollars worth of Ether. The incident raised questions about the security and governance of DAOs and led to a hard fork of the Ethereum blockchain to reverse the effects of the hack. Since then, DAO developers and participants have implemented various security measures and best practices to prevent similar incidents from occurring in the future.

Regulatory challenges and legal considerations present additional hurdles for the adoption and mainstream acceptance of DAOs. As decentralized and borderless entities, DAOs operate outside the traditional regulatory framework, raising questions about jurisdiction, accountability, and compliance. Regulators around the world are grappling with how to classify and regulate DAOs, with some countries taking a proactive approach to provide clarity and guidance, while others are adopting a wait-and-see approach to monitor developments and assess risks.

Despite these challenges, DAOs hold immense promise for democratizing access to financial services, empowering communities, and fostering innovation. By leveraging blockchain technology and smart contracts, DAOs offer a new model for organizing and coordinating collective action in a decentralized and transparent manner. As the technology matures and regulatory frameworks evolve, we can expect to see DAOs play an increasingly important role in shaping the future of governance, finance, and beyond.

DAOs represent a groundbreaking innovation in organizational governance and decision-making, with the potential to revolutionize how we collaborate, coordinate, and govern in the digital age. While DAOs face challenges and uncertainties, they also offer unprecedented opportunities for decentralization, transparency, and participation in the global economy. As DAOs continue to evolve and gain traction, it will be essential for developers, participants, and regulators to work together to address concerns, mitigate risks, and unlock the full potential of decentralized autonomous organizations.

Chapter Five

The Intersection of AI and Blockchain: Exploring Synergies

Harnessing artificial intelligence (AI) for predictive analytics in cryptocurrency trading has become increasingly prevalent in recent years. AI algorithms analyze vast amounts of historical and real-time data to identify patterns, trends, and anomalies in cryptocurrency markets, enabling traders to make informed decisions and execute profitable trades. By leveraging machine learning techniques such as neural networks and deep learning, AI-powered trading bots can adapt and evolve over time, continually improving their predictive accuracy and performance in dynamic market conditions.

AI-driven smart contracts and automated governance systems are revolutionizing the way decentralized autonomous organizations (DAOs) operate. Smart contracts, which are self-executing contracts with the terms of the agreement directly written into code, can automate and enforce rules and agreements within DAOs, reducing the need for manual intervention and increasing efficiency and transparency. Automated governance systems use AI algorithms to facilitate decision-making processes within DAOs, enabling participants to vote on proposals, allocate resources, and govern the organization in a decentralized and democratic manner.

However, the integration of AI and blockchain technology also presents ethical implications and challenges that must be carefully considered. One of the main concerns is the potential for bias and discrimination in AI algorithms, which can perpetuate existing inequalities and reinforce systemic biases. As AI-powered systems become increasingly autonomous and decentralized, ensuring fairness, transparency, and accountability in decision-making processes becomes critical to mitigating these risks and promoting ethical AI-Blockchain integration.

Another ethical concern is the potential for AI-driven smart contracts to execute malicious or unintended actions autonomously. Smart contracts are immutable and irreversible once deployed on the blockchain, meaning that errors or vulnerabilities in the code can have significant consequences. As smart contracts become more complex and interconnected, ensuring the security and reliability of these systems becomes paramount to protecting users and minimizing the risk of exploitation or manipulation.

Additionally, the use of AI in cryptocurrency trading and governance systems raises questions about privacy and data protection. AI algorithms rely on vast amounts of data to train and operate effectively, raising concerns about the privacy and security of personal and sensitive information stored on blockchain networks. As regulators grapple with how to address these concerns, developers and organizations must implement robust privacy measures and compliance protocols to protect user data and ensure compliance with applicable regulations.

The integration of AI and blockchain technology holds immense promise for transforming various industries and applications, from cryptocurrency trading to decentralized governance. By harnessing the power of AI for predictive analytics, smart contracts, and governance systems, organizations can unlock new opportunities for efficiency, transparency, and innovation. However, it is essential to address the ethical implications and challenges of AI-Blockchain integration, including bias, security, privacy, and accountability, to ensure that these technologies are used responsibly and ethically for the benefit of society.

Cryptocurrency in Emerging Markets: Opportunities and Challenges

Adoption trends in developing economies provide valuable insights into the potential of cryptocurrency to transform financial systems and empower underserved communities. Case studies from Africa, Asia, and Latin America highlight the diverse ways in which cryptocurrencies are being used to address economic challenges and promote financial inclusion. In countries with limited access to traditional banking services, cryptocurrencies offer a lifeline, enabling individuals to send and receive money, access credit, and participate in the global economy from their mobile devices.

Bridging the digital divide is a key objective of many cryptocurrency initiatives in developing economies. Mobile payments have emerged as a powerful tool for expanding financial inclusion, allowing individuals without access to traditional banking services to participate in the digital economy. Mobile money platforms, such as M-Pesa in Kenya and Paytm in India, have revolutionized the way people send and receive money, pay bills, and access financial services, providing a blueprint for leveraging technology to bridge the gap between the unbanked and the traditional financial system.

However, regulatory hurdles pose significant challenges to the adoption and growth of cryptocurrency in emerging markets. Governments and regulators in these countries are grappling with how to regulate and oversee cryptocurrency transactions while balancing concerns about consumer protection, financial stability, and illicit activities. In some cases, regulatory uncertainty and ambiguity have stifled innovation and investment in the cryptocurrency sector, limiting its potential to drive economic growth and development.

The socioeconomic impact of cryptocurrency in emerging markets is complex and multifaceted. On one hand, cryptocurrency has the potential to empower individuals and communities by providing access to financial services and economic opportunities. By reducing the cost and friction of financial transactions, cryptocurrencies can enable entrepreneurs to access capital, workers to send remittances, and consumers to make purchases more efficiently. On the other hand, cryptocurrency also poses risks, including volatility, fraud, and security concerns, which can disproportionately affect vulnerable populations and exacerbate existing socioeconomic inequalities.

In Africa, for example, cryptocurrency adoption is growing rapidly, driven by factors such as high mobile penetration, limited access to traditional banking services, and a young and tech-savvy population. Countries like Nigeria, Kenya, and South Africa have seen a surge in cryptocurrency trading and investment, with individuals using digital assets for remittances, savings, and investments. However, regulatory uncertainty and lack of consumer protection have hampered the growth of the cryptocurrency sector in some African countries, highlighting the need for clear and consistent regulatory frameworks to support innovation and protect users.

In Asia, cryptocurrency adoption varies widely across countries, with some embracing digital assets as a means of financial inclusion and economic empowerment, while others remain skeptical or hostile towards cryptocurrencies. In countries like India and China, regulatory crackdowns and restrictions on cryptocurrency trading and mining have dampened enthusiasm for digital assets, despite their potential to address financial inclusion challenges and stimulate economic growth. However, other countries in the region, such as Singapore and Japan, have adopted more favorable regulatory approaches, fostering innovation and investment in the cryptocurrency sector.

In Latin America, cryptocurrency adoption is also on the rise, driven by factors such as hyperinflation, economic instability, and limited access to traditional banking services. Countries like Venezuela and Argentina have seen growing interest in cryptocurrencies as a hedge against inflation and a means of preserving wealth in the face of economic uncertainty. However, regulatory uncertainty and concerns about money laundering and fraud have posed challenges to the growth of the cryptocurrency sector in the region, underscoring the need for clear and effective regulatory frameworks to support responsible innovation and protect consumers.

Adoption trends in developing economies provide valuable insights into the potential of cryptocurrency to drive financial inclusion and economic empowerment. By leveraging mobile payments, addressing regulatory hurdles, and understanding the socioeconomic impact of cryptocurrency, policymakers, entrepreneurs, and investors can harness the transformative power of digital assets to create a more inclusive and resilient financial system for all.

Sustainable Cryptocurrency: Environmental Solutions and Green Initiatives

The carbon footprint of cryptocurrency mining has become a pressing concern in recent years, as the energy consumption associated with mining operations continues to rise. Cryptocurrency mining, which involves solving complex mathematical puzzles to validate transactions and secure the network, requires significant computational power and energy consumption, primarily from fossil fuel sources. The environmental impact of mining has led to growing calls for sustainable solutions to reduce energy consumption and mitigate the carbon footprint of cryptocurrency.

Renewable energy solutions offer a promising avenue for reducing the environmental impact of cryptocurrency mining operations. By harnessing renewable energy sources such as solar, wind, and hydroelectric power, mining operations can reduce their reliance on fossil fuels and lower their carbon emissions. Countries with abundant renewable energy resources, such as Iceland and Norway, have become popular destinations for cryptocurrency mining operations due to their low-cost and renewable energy sources.

Eco-friendly blockchain projects and carbon offsetting initiatives are also emerging as effective strategies for mitigating the environmental impact of cryptocurrency. Some blockchain projects are exploring alternative consensus mechanisms that require less energy than traditional proof-of-work mining, such as proof-of-stake or proof-of-authority. These projects aim to reduce the energy consumption and carbon emissions associated with mining while maintaining the security and decentralization of the blockchain network.

Carbon offsetting initiatives allow cryptocurrency mining operations to offset their carbon emissions by investing in projects that reduce or remove greenhouse gas emissions from the atmosphere. These projects may include reforestation, renewable energy development, or methane capture initiatives, which help to offset the carbon emissions generated by mining activities. By participating in carbon offsetting initiatives, cryptocurrency mining operations can mitigate their environmental impact and contribute to global efforts to combat climate change.

In addition to renewable energy solutions and carbon offsetting initiatives, technological innovations such as energy-efficient mining hardware and cooling systems are also helping to reduce the energy consumption of cryptocurrency mining. Manufacturers are developing more energy-efficient ASIC miners and GPUs, which consume less power while delivering comparable or improved performance. Similarly, innovative cooling solutions, such as immersion cooling and liquid cooling systems, help to dissipate heat more efficiently, reducing the energy required to cool mining hardware.

Despite these efforts, addressing the carbon footprint of cryptocurrency mining remains a complex and multifaceted challenge. The decentralized nature of blockchain networks and the global distribution of mining operations make it difficult to implement uniform regulations or mandates to reduce energy consumption. Moreover, the profitability of mining operations often depends on factors such as energy costs and regulatory environments, which can vary significantly from one region to another.

However, with growing awareness of the environmental impact of cryptocurrency mining and increasing pressure from stakeholders to adopt sustainable practices, the industry is gradually moving towards greener and more eco-friendly solutions. By embracing renewable energy, participating in carbon offsetting initiatives, and investing in energy-efficient technologies, cryptocurrency mining operations can reduce their carbon footprint and contribute to a more sustainable future for blockchain technology.

Chapter Six

Privacy Coins and the Quest for Financial Privacy

The rise of privacy-centric cryptocurrencies has emerged as a response to growing concerns about privacy and anonymity in the digital economy. Coins like Monero, Zcash, and Dash offer users enhanced privacy features, such as confidential transactions and anonymous addresses, that shield their financial transactions from prying eyes. These privacy coins have gained popularity among users seeking to protect their financial privacy and maintain anonymity in an increasingly surveilled and transparent financial landscape.

Privacy coins provide users with a level of financial privacy and anonymity that traditional cryptocurrencies like Bitcoin cannot offer. By obfuscating transaction details, such as sender and recipient addresses and transaction amounts, privacy coins prevent third parties from tracking and analyzing users' financial activities. This privacy-enhancing feature is particularly appealing to individuals and businesses that value confidentiality and discretion in their financial transactions.

However, the rise of privacy-centric cryptocurrencies has also raised concerns among regulators and law enforcement agencies about the potential for illicit activities, such as money laundering, tax evasion, and terrorism financing. The anonymity provided by privacy coins makes it difficult for authorities to track and trace suspicious transactions, raising questions about how to balance privacy and regulatory compliance in the digital economy.

Privacy vs. regulatory compliance is a delicate balance that cryptocurrency projects and users must navigate carefully. While privacy coins offer enhanced privacy features that protect users' financial privacy and anonymity, they also pose challenges for regulatory compliance and law enforcement efforts. Regulators and policymakers are grappling with how to regulate privacy coins effectively without stifling innovation or infringing on individuals' rights to financial privacy.

Despite these challenges, privacy coins have found various use cases in the digital economy. For example, privacy coins are often used for peer-to-peer transactions, online purchases, and remittances, where users value privacy and anonymity. Businesses and individuals may also use privacy coins to protect sensitive financial information from hackers, data breaches, and surveillance. Additionally, privacy coins have gained traction in industries such as gaming, gambling, and adult entertainment, where users may prefer to keep their financial transactions private.

Moreover, privacy coins are increasingly being integrated into decentralized finance (DeFi) platforms and applications, where they offer users enhanced privacy and security for financial transactions and interactions. DeFi projects built on privacy coins enable users to access financial services such as lending, borrowing, and trading while preserving their financial privacy and anonymity. These projects leverage the privacy features of privacy coins to protect users' sensitive financial data and transactions from surveillance and exploitation.

The rise of privacy-centric cryptocurrencies like Monero, Zcash, and Dash reflects a growing demand for financial privacy and anonymity in the digital economy. While privacy coins offer users enhanced privacy features and anonymity, they also pose challenges for regulatory compliance and law enforcement efforts. However, privacy coins have found various use cases in the digital economy, from peer-to-peer transactions and online purchases to decentralized finance (DeFi) applications. As privacy coins continue to evolve and gain adoption, it will be essential to strike a balance between privacy and regulatory compliance to ensure the integrity and security of the digital financial system.

Decentralized Identity and Self-Sovereign Identity (SSI)

Identity plays a crucial role in the digital age, where individuals interact with various online platforms and services on a daily basis. From social media accounts to online banking, identity verification is essential for establishing trust, security, and accountability in digital transactions and interactions. However, traditional identity systems are often centralized, fragmented, and vulnerable to data breaches and identity theft, raising concerns about privacy, security, and control over personal information.

Self-sovereign identity solutions offer a revolutionary approach to identity management, empowering individuals to own, control, and manage their digital identities without relying on intermediaries or central authorities. With self-sovereign identity solutions, individuals can securely store their identity information, such as biometric data, personal documents, and credentials, on their devices or in decentralized storage systems, such as blockchain networks. By leveraging cryptographic techniques and decentralized technologies, self-sovereign identity solutions enable individuals to assert their identity and authenticate themselves without disclosing unnecessary personal information, enhancing privacy, security, and control over their digital identities.

The applications of decentralized identity extend far beyond traditional identity verification use cases. In the healthcare sector, decentralized identity solutions enable patients to securely access and share their medical records with healthcare providers, researchers, and other stakeholders, improving interoperability, privacy, and security in healthcare data management. By giving patients greater control over their medical information, decentralized identity solutions empower individuals to make informed decisions about their health and participate more actively in their care.

Similarly, decentralized identity solutions have the potential to transform the voting process, making it more secure, transparent, and accessible. By enabling individuals to verify their identity and cast their votes securely and anonymously using their digital identities, decentralized identity solutions can reduce the risk of voter fraud, enhance election integrity, and increase voter turnout. Moreover, decentralized identity solutions can facilitate remote and mobile voting, enabling individuals to participate in elections from anywhere in the world, thereby promoting inclusivity and democracy.

Beyond healthcare and voting, decentralized identity solutions have numerous other applications in various industries and use cases. For example, decentralized identity can be used to streamline identity verification processes in financial services, enabling individuals to open bank accounts, apply for loans, and access financial services more quickly and securely. In education, decentralized identity solutions can provide students with secure digital credentials, such as diplomas and certificates, that are tamper-proof and verifiable, enhancing the trust and authenticity of academic credentials.

Furthermore, decentralized identity solutions can be used to address identity-related challenges in humanitarian aid and refugee resettlement, where individuals may lack reliable identity documents or face obstacles to accessing essential services. By providing individuals with portable and verifiable digital identities, decentralized identity solutions can enable humanitarian organizations and governments to deliver aid and services more efficiently and effectively to those in need.

Decentralized identity solutions offer a transformative approach to identity management, empowering individuals to own, control, and manage their digital identities in the digital age. With applications in healthcare, voting, financial services, education, and beyond, decentralized identity solutions have the potential to revolutionize how we verify identity, access services, and interact online, ultimately fostering a more secure, transparent, and inclusive digital society.

Exploring Cross-Chain Interoperability

Blockchain silos pose a significant challenge to the widespread adoption and scalability of blockchain technology. As blockchain networks continue to proliferate, each with its own set of protocols, consensus mechanisms, and native assets, interoperability becomes increasingly crucial for enabling seamless communication and value transfer between disparate blockchains. Interoperability protocols and cross-chain bridges offer innovative solutions to overcome blockchain silos, allowing different blockchain networks to interoperate and exchange data and assets securely and efficiently.

Projects like Polkadot, Cosmos, and others are leading the charge in developing interoperability solutions to bridge the gap between blockchain networks. Polkadot, for example, is a multi-chain framework that enables different blockchains to connect and share information, assets, and functionality through a unified network. By providing interoperability between diverse blockchains, Polkadot aims to create a scalable and interconnected ecosystem where developers can build and deploy decentralized applications (dApps) with ease.

Similarly, Cosmos is a decentralized network of independent blockchains, known as zones, that are interoperable with each other through the Cosmos Hub. Cosmos uses the Inter-Blockchain Communication (IBC) protocol to enable secure and trustless communication and asset transfer between different blockchains. With Cosmos, developers can create custom blockchains tailored to specific use cases and connect them to the broader Cosmos network, unlocking new possibilities for cross-chain interoperability and collaboration.

These interoperability projects are not only breaking down barriers between blockchain networks but also unlocking the potential of decentralized finance (DeFi) by enabling cross-chain compatibility. DeFi refers to a set of financial services and applications built on blockchain technology, such as lending, borrowing, trading, and asset management, that operate without intermediaries or centralized authorities. However, the fragmented nature of blockchain ecosystems has hindered the growth of DeFi by limiting interoperability between different blockchain networks.

With cross-chain compatibility enabled by interoperability protocols and cross-chain bridges, DeFi applications can access a broader range of assets, liquidity pools, and users across multiple blockchain networks. For example, decentralized exchanges (DEXs) can offer liquidity pools that span multiple blockchains, allowing users to trade assets seamlessly between different networks. Similarly, lending and borrowing protocols can support cross-chain collateralization, enabling users to borrow assets against their holdings on different blockchains.

By facilitating cross-chain interoperability, projects like Polkadot, Cosmos, and others are driving innovation and collaboration in the DeFi space, enabling developers to build more robust and interconnected financial applications. With interoperability, DeFi platforms can achieve greater scalability, liquidity, and composability, unlocking new opportunities for financial inclusion, innovation, and value creation in the decentralized economy.

Overcoming blockchain silos through interoperability protocols and cross-chain bridges is essential for realizing the full potential of blockchain technology and decentralized finance. Projects like Polkadot and Cosmos are pioneering interoperability solutions that enable different blockchain networks to interoperate and collaborate seamlessly, unlocking new possibilities for cross-chain compatibility and innovation in the DeFi space. As interoperability continues to evolve, we can expect to see a more interconnected and interoperable blockchain ecosystem that fosters greater collaboration, efficiency, and resilience in the decentralized economy.

Chapter Seven

Quantum Computing and the Future of Cryptography

The rise of quantum computing poses a significant threat to traditional cryptography, which relies on mathematical algorithms that are vulnerable to attacks from quantum computers. Unlike classical computers, which use bits to represent data as either 0 or 1, quantum computers leverage quantum bits, or qubits, which can exist in multiple states simultaneously, allowing them to perform complex calculations at an exponentially faster rate. This exponential increase in computational power enables quantum computers to break cryptographic algorithms that are currently considered secure, such as RSA and ECC, by leveraging algorithms like Shor's algorithm.

To address the threat posed by quantum computing, researchers and cryptographers are developing post-quantum cryptography, which aims to create cryptographic protocols and algorithms that are resistant to attacks from quantum computers. These quantum-resistant algorithms are designed to withstand quantum attacks and maintain the confidentiality, integrity, and authenticity of digital communications and transactions in the post-quantum era. Post-quantum cryptography encompasses a wide range of cryptographic primitives, including digital signatures, encryption schemes, and key exchange protocols, each designed to provide quantum-resistant security guarantees.

Collaborative efforts and research in quantum-safe cryptography are underway to develop and standardize quantum-resistant cryptographic algorithms that can be deployed across various systems and applications. Organizations such as the National Institute of

Standards and Technology (NIST) are leading the charge in soliciting, evaluating, and standardizing post-quantum cryptographic algorithms through open competitions and collaborative processes involving researchers, academics, industry experts, and government agencies. These efforts aim to establish a new generation of cryptographic standards that can withstand the capabilities of quantum computers and ensure the long-term security of digital communications and transactions.

One approach to post-quantum cryptography involves lattice-based cryptography, which relies on the hardness of certain lattice problems to provide security against quantum attacks. Lattice-based cryptographic algorithms, such as the Learning With Errors (LWE) problem and the Ring-LWE problem, offer strong security guarantees and are considered among the most promising candidates for post-quantum cryptography. These algorithms form the basis of cryptographic primitives such as digital signatures, encryption schemes, and key exchange protocols that are resistant to attacks from quantum computers.

Another approach to post-quantum cryptography involves code-based cryptography, which leverages error-correcting codes to provide security against quantum attacks. Code-based cryptographic algorithms, such as the McEliece cryptosystem, rely on the difficulty of decoding linear codes to provide quantum-resistant security guarantees. Despite their relatively large key sizes and computational overhead, code-based cryptographic algorithms offer robust security properties and are considered viable candidates for post-quantum cryptography in certain applications.

And also to lattice-based and code-based cryptography, other approaches to post-quantum cryptography include hash-based cryptography, multivariate polynomial cryptography, and isogeny-based cryptography, each offering unique security properties and trade-offs. By diversifying the cryptographic toolkit with quantum-resistant algorithms, researchers aim to future-proof digital communications and transactions against the threat posed by quantum computing, ensuring the long-term security and integrity of the digital infrastructure. Through collaborative efforts and ongoing research, the cryptographic community is working towards a quantum-safe future where digital security remains resilient in the face of advancing technology.

Social Impact of Cryptocurrency Philanthropy and Community Building

Cryptocurrency has emerged as a powerful tool for charitable giving, enabling individuals and organizations to support causes and make a positive impact on society. Through case studies and initiatives, we see how cryptocurrency is being used to address various social and humanitarian issues, from poverty and hunger to education and healthcare. Cryptocurrency donations offer several advantages over traditional forms of giving, including lower transaction fees, greater transparency, and faster cross-border transactions, making it easier for donors to support causes they care about and for charitable organizations to receive and distribute funds efficiently.

In addition to charitable giving, cryptocurrency is also being used to build resilient communities through crowdfunding, mutual aid, and disaster relief efforts. Crowdfunding platforms powered by cryptocurrency allow individuals and organizations to raise funds for projects, initiatives, and causes directly from their supporters, bypassing traditional financial intermediaries and gatekeepers. Mutual aid networks, fueled by cryptocurrency donations, enable community members to support each other during times of crisis, providing financial assistance, resources, and solidarity to those in need. Moreover, cryptocurrency is playing a crucial role in disaster relief efforts, enabling donors to send funds quickly and securely to affected areas, where traditional banking infrastructure may be disrupted or inaccessible.

However, harnessing cryptocurrency for social good also presents challenges and opportunities that must be addressed to maximize its impact. One challenge is ensuring the accountability, transparency, and effectiveness of cryptocurrency donations, as the decentralized and pseudonymous nature of blockchain transactions can make it difficult to track and verify the use of funds. Additionally, regulatory uncertainty, technological barriers, and security concerns may deter donors and charitable organizations from embracing cryptocurrency as a fundraising and donation mechanism.

Despite these challenges, there are significant opportunities to leverage cryptocurrency for social good and create positive change in communities around the world. For example, cryptocurrency can empower individuals and communities to take control of their financial destinies, bypassing traditional financial institutions and intermediaries and reducing dependence on centralized systems. By providing access to financial services and resources, cryptocurrency has the potential to uplift marginalized and underserved populations, promoting financial inclusion, economic empowerment, and social equity.

Moreover, cryptocurrency can facilitate cross-border giving and international cooperation, enabling donors and organizations to support causes and communities beyond their geographical boundaries. Cryptocurrency donations can reach remote and underserved areas where traditional banking infrastructure is lacking, enabling faster and more efficient aid delivery in times of crisis. Furthermore, cryptocurrency can catalyze innovation and collaboration in the nonprofit sector, inspiring new fundraising models, partnerships, and initiatives that leverage blockchain technology and digital currencies to drive social impact.

Cryptocurrency has the potential to revolutionize charitable giving and community resilience, offering new opportunities to address social, economic, and environmental challenges worldwide. By supporting initiatives and organizations that harness cryptocurrency for social good, individuals can contribute to positive change and make a difference in the lives of others. While challenges remain, the transformative potential of cryptocurrency for social good is undeniable, paving the way for a more inclusive, equitable, and resilient future for all.

The Evolution of Central Bank Digital Currencies (CBDCs)

Central Bank Digital Currencies (CBDCs) have garnered significant attention as central banks around the world explore the potential benefits and implications of issuing digital currencies. Understanding CBDCs requires examining the different approaches taken by central banks, ranging from centralized to decentralized models. While some central banks are exploring centralized CBDCs, which would be issued and regulated by a central authority, others are considering decentralized CBDCs, which would leverage blockchain technology and distributed ledger technology (DLT) to enable peer-to-peer transactions without the need for intermediaries.

Global trends in CBDC development offer valuable insights into the various approaches and strategies adopted by central banks in different countries. China, for example, has emerged as a leader in CBDC development, with the People's Bank of China (PBOC) piloting its digital currency, the Digital Currency Electronic Payment (DCEP), in several cities. The DCEP aims to enhance financial inclusion, reduce transaction costs, and improve the efficiency of payment systems in China. Similarly, Sweden is exploring the issuance of an e-krona as a response to the declining use of cash and the rise of digital payments in the country. The Bahamas has also launched its digital currency, the Sand Dollar, to address financial inclusion and promote digital payments in the archipelago.

The development of CBDCs has significant implications for monetary policy, financial stability, and economic sovereignty. Central banks are grappling with complex issues related to the design, implementation, and governance of CBDCs, including monetary control, financial stability, privacy, security, and regulatory compliance. CBDCs have the potential to transform the way monetary policy is conducted, as central banks gain greater visibility and control over money supply, payment systems, and financial transactions. However, CBDCs also pose challenges in terms of financial stability, as they could disrupt traditional banking systems and payment networks, leading to potential risks such as bank disintermediation, liquidity crises, and cyber threats.

Moreover, CBDCs raise questions about economic sovereignty and the role of central banks in the digital age. While CBDCs offer central banks an opportunity to maintain control over the monetary system and currency issuance, they also pose challenges to existing monetary and financial structures. Central banks must strike a balance between innovation and stability, ensuring that CBDCs promote financial inclusion, innovation, and efficiency while mitigating risks and safeguarding the integrity of the financial system.

Understanding CBDCs requires considering the different approaches taken by central banks, analyzing global trends in CBDC development, and assessing the implications for monetary policy, financial stability, and economic sovereignty. While CBDCs offer promising opportunities to enhance financial inclusion, efficiency, and innovation, they also pose challenges in terms of design, implementation, and governance. Central banks must navigate these challenges carefully, leveraging CBDCs to promote the public interest and ensure the stability and resilience of the financial system in the digital age.

Chapter Eight

Regenerative Finance: Blockchain Solutions for Environmental Conservation

Green blockchain initiatives are gaining momentum as the world grapples with the urgent need to address climate change and environmental degradation. These initiatives leverage blockchain technology to promote sustainability, reduce carbon emissions, and support environmental conservation efforts. One approach involves carbon offsetting, where blockchain platforms facilitate the trading of carbon credits, enabling individuals and organizations to invest in projects that mitigate or offset their carbon footprint. By tokenizing carbon credits on the blockchain, these initiatives aim to create transparent and efficient markets for carbon trading, incentivizing investments in renewable energy, energy efficiency, and reforestation projects.

Sustainable supply chains are another focus area for green blockchain initiatives, aiming to increase transparency and traceability in global supply chains to reduce environmental impact and promote ethical practices. Blockchain platforms enable stakeholders to track and verify the origin, production, and transportation of goods and raw materials, ensuring compliance with sustainability standards and reducing the risk of deforestation, habitat destruction, and pollution. By promoting transparency and accountability, blockchain technology empowers consumers to make informed choices and support environmentally responsible businesses and products.

Tokenized ecosystems offer innovative solutions for environmental conservation, enabling individuals and organizations to invest in and support initiatives such as wildlife protection, ocean cleanup, and climate action through digital tokens and decentralized platforms. These initiatives tokenize natural assets, such as forests, wildlife habitats, and marine ecosystems, allowing investors to contribute to conservation efforts and receive rewards or incentives in return. By leveraging blockchain technology, tokenized ecosystems provide new opportunities for funding, collaboration, and impact measurement in environmental conservation, empowering communities and stakeholders to participate in conservation efforts and protect biodiversity.

Collaborations between blockchain projects, non-governmental organizations (NGOs), and governments are essential for advancing green blockchain initiatives and scaling their impact. These partnerships bring together diverse expertise, resources, and networks to address complex environmental challenges and implement innovative solutions. NGOs and governments provide domain knowledge, regulatory guidance, and funding support, while blockchain projects offer technological expertise, innovation, and scalability. Together, these stakeholders can design and implement green blockchain initiatives that drive meaningful change and contribute to global efforts to achieve environmental sustainability and climate resilience.

Green blockchain initiatives hold immense potential to address environmental challenges and promote sustainability by leveraging blockchain technology to facilitate carbon offsetting, sustainable supply chains, tokenized ecosystems, and collaborative partnerships. These initiatives offer innovative solutions to mitigate climate change, protect ecosystems, and promote responsible stewardship of natural resources. By harnessing the power of blockchain technology and fostering collaborations between stakeholders, we can create a more sustainable and resilient future for generations to come.

The Future of Work: Decentralized Autonomous Workforces (DAWs)

The emergence of Gig Economy 2.0 brings forth decentralized freelancing platforms and autonomous organizations, transforming the way people work and collaborate in the digital age. These platforms leverage blockchain technology to create decentralized marketplaces where freelancers and clients can connect and transact directly, without the need for intermediaries or centralized authorities. By eliminating intermediaries, decentralized freelancing platforms offer greater transparency, lower fees, and increased autonomy for freelancers, enabling them to retain a larger share of their earnings and have more control over their work.

Decentralized Autonomous Organizations (DAOs) are at the forefront of decentralized governance and decision-making in corporate structures, enabling stakeholders to participate in collective decision-making processes and govern organizations in a transparent and decentralized manner. DAOs leverage blockchain technology and smart contracts to automate decision-making, voting, and resource allocation, enabling stakeholders to contribute to the governance of organizations and participate in profit-sharing and incentive mechanisms. By decentralizing governance, DAOs aim to create more inclusive, resilient, and equitable organizational structures that empower stakeholders and align incentives for collective success.

The rise of Gig Economy 2.0 and DAOs has significant implications for labor rights, employment regulations, and income distribution. As traditional employment models give way to decentralized freelancing platforms and autonomous organizations, questions arise about the rights and protections afforded to workers in the digital economy. Freelancers may face challenges such as lack of access to benefits, job insecurity, and income volatility, highlighting the need for new regulations and policies to address the evolving nature of work in the gig economy. Similarly, the rise of DAOs raises questions about corporate governance, liability, and accountability, as stakeholders navigate the legal and regulatory landscape surrounding decentralized organizations.

Despite these challenges, Gig Economy 2.0 and DAOs offer opportunities to reimagine labor relations, employment structures, and income distribution in the digital age. Decentralized freelancing platforms empower freelancers to access global markets, collaborate with clients around the world, and build their professional reputations without relying on traditional intermediaries. Similarly, DAOs enable stakeholders to participate in the governance and decision-making of organizations, aligning incentives and fostering greater transparency, accountability, and trust in corporate structures. By embracing decentralized technologies and innovative organizational models, we can create a more inclusive, resilient, and equitable future of work for all stakeholders.

Gig Economy 2.0 and DAOs represent a paradigm shift in how work is organized, governed, and compensated in the digital economy. Decentralized freelancing platforms empower freelancers to work on their own terms, while DAOs enable stakeholders to participate in the governance of organizations in a transparent and decentralized manner. While these developments present challenges in terms of labor rights, regulations, and income distribution, they also offer opportunities to create more inclusive, resilient, and equitable systems of work and governance. By embracing decentralized technologies and collaborative organizational models, we can unlock the full potential of the digital economy and create opportunities for prosperity and innovation for all stakeholders.

Web3: Building the Decentralized Internet of the Future

The fundamentals of Web3 lay the groundwork for a decentralized internet, characterized by decentralized protocols, peer-to-peer networks, and individual data ownership. Unlike the centralized model of Web2, where data is stored on centralized servers owned by corporations, Web3 operates on decentralized protocols such as blockchain and peer-to-peer networks, enabling users to interact directly without intermediaries. Moreover, in the Web3 paradigm, individuals have greater control over their data, with ownership and control resting in the hands of users rather than centralized platforms.

The applications of Web3 technologies span various sectors, including decentralized social media, file storage, and content distribution. Decentralized social media platforms leverage blockchain technology to create censorship-resistant and privacy-enhancing alternatives to traditional social media platforms. By decentralizing data storage and governance, these platforms enable users to control their data, protect their privacy, and participate in community-driven decision-making processes. Similarly, decentralized file storage and content distribution networks offer secure, efficient, and censorship-resistant alternatives to centralized cloud storage and content delivery networks, enabling users to store and share data in a decentralized and peer-to-peer manner.

Transitioning to a decentralized web presents both challenges and opportunities for individuals, businesses, and society as a whole. One challenge is the technical complexity and scalability limitations of Web3 technologies, which require robust infrastructure and development frameworks to support widespread adoption and usage. Moreover, transitioning to a decentralized web requires overcoming regulatory, legal, and governance challenges, as existing laws and regulations may not adequately address the unique characteristics and implications of decentralized technologies. Additionally, transitioning to a decentralized web requires addressing concerns related to interoperability, user experience, and network security to ensure a seamless and secure user experience.

Despite these challenges, transitioning to a decentralized web offers significant opportunities to reshape the internet and empower users with greater control, privacy, and sovereignty over their data and digital identities. By decentralizing data storage, governance, and control, Web3 technologies enable users to break free from the grip of centralized platforms and regain ownership of their digital lives. Moreover, transitioning to a decentralized web has the potential to foster innovation, competition, and diversity in the digital ecosystem, as decentralized protocols and platforms enable permissionless innovation and open access to resources and markets.

Web3 represents a paradigm shift in how we conceive and interact with the internet, offering a decentralized alternative to the centralized model of Web2. By leveraging decentralized protocols, peer-to-peer networks, and individual data ownership, Web3 technologies empower users with greater control, privacy, and sovereignty over their digital lives. While transitioning to a decentralized web presents challenges, such as technical complexity, regulatory uncertainty, and interoperability issues, it also offers opportunities to reshape the internet and create a more open, inclusive, and resilient digital ecosystem for all.

Chapter Nine

The Metaverse Economy: Virtual Assets and Digital Realities

In the vast expanse of the digital realm, where reality intertwines seamlessly with the virtual, lies a bustling marketplace known as the Metaverse. Here, the concept of ownership takes on a new form, transcending physical boundaries and manifesting in the realm of NFTs and virtual land. As we delve deeper into this virtual universe, we uncover a tapestry woven with threads of innovation, economic evolution, and social transformation.

NFTs, or Non-Fungible Tokens, have emerged as the cornerstone of digital ownership within the Metaverse. These unique digital assets, built on blockchain technology, represent ownership of digital goods ranging from artwork to virtual real estate. With each NFT possessing distinct attributes and provenance, they imbue digital assets with scarcity, rarity, and value, mirroring the dynamics of the physical world.

Virtual land ownership stands at the forefront of this digital revolution, offering individuals the opportunity to claim their stake in the Metaverse. In virtual worlds such as Decentraland and The Sandbox, parcels of virtual land are bought, sold, and developed, mirroring the dynamics of real-world real estate markets. However, unlike traditional property ownership, virtual land grants its owners boundless creative freedom, enabling them to build and monetize digital experiences limited only by their imagination.

The integration of cryptocurrencies within the Metaverse further blurs the lines between the physical and digital worlds. In virtual economies, cryptocurrencies serve as the primary medium of exchange, facilitating seamless transactions within virtual marketplaces. From purchasing virtual goods to investing in virtual assets, cryptocurrencies have become the lifeblood of the Metaverse economy, driving innovation and economic growth within digital communities.

Yet, as the Metaverse economy continues to evolve, it brings forth a myriad of legal, social, and economic implications that warrant careful consideration. From the enforcement of intellectual property rights to the regulation of virtual currencies, policymakers grapple with the challenges of governing a decentralized and borderless digital realm. Moreover, the social dynamics within the Metaverse raise questions surrounding identity, privacy, and community governance, prompting discussions on the ethical implications of virtual interactions.

Amidst these complexities, the Metaverse presents a landscape ripe with opportunities for innovation and exploration. Entrepreneurs and developers flock to this digital frontier, seeking to carve out their niche and shape the future of virtual commerce. With each new innovation and technological advancement, the boundaries of the Metaverse expand, offering glimpses of a future where the physical and digital worlds converge seamlessly.

As we navigate the intricacies of the Metaverse marketplace, we are confronted with a myriad of possibilities and challenges that transcend traditional notions of ownership and commerce. In this boundless digital landscape, the lines between reality and fantasy blur, giving rise to a new era of creativity, collaboration, and economic prosperity. As pioneers of this digital frontier, we stand at the precipice of a transformative journey, where the boundaries of possibility are limited only by our imagination.

Quantum Blockchain: Securing the Future of Cryptocurrency

In the ever-evolving landscape of blockchain technology, a new frontier emerges: quantum security. As quantum computing capabilities advance, traditional cryptographic protocols face unprecedented threats. To combat this looming challenge, researchers and developers are pioneering quantum-secure blockchain solutions, ushering in a new era of cryptographic resilience and digital security.

At the heart of this endeavor lies post-quantum cryptography, a branch of cryptography dedicated to developing algorithms resistant to quantum attacks. Unlike classical cryptographic schemes, which rely on the hardness of mathematical problems such as factoring large integers or computing discrete logarithms, post-quantum cryptography harnesses the power of mathematical constructs immune to quantum algorithms. From lattice-based cryptography to hash-based signatures, these novel cryptographic primitives form the cornerstone of quantum-resilient blockchain protocols.

In parallel, quantum-resistant algorithms are garnering attention for their ability to withstand the computational power of quantum adversaries. Leveraging mathematical structures resistant to quantum algorithms, such as multivariate polynomial equations and code-based cryptography, these algorithms offer a robust defense against quantum attacks. By integrating quantum-resistant algorithms into blockchain protocols, developers can fortify the security of decentralized networks against the looming threat of quantum computing.

Furthermore, quantum key distribution (QKD) emerges as a promising avenue for securing blockchain transactions in the quantum era. Unlike classical key exchange protocols vulnerable to eavesdropping attacks facilitated by quantum computers, QKD offers a provably secure method for establishing cryptographic keys over quantum channels. Through the principles of quantum mechanics, QKD enables parties to exchange encryption keys with unprecedented security, laying the foundation for quantum-secure blockchain transactions.

Collaborative efforts in quantum blockchain research and development are paramount to advancing the frontier of quantum security. Across academia, industry, and government sectors, researchers collaborate to explore novel cryptographic primitives, develop quantum-resistant algorithms, and implement quantum-safe protocols within blockchain ecosystems. Through open collaboration and knowledge sharing, these interdisciplinary initiatives foster innovation and accelerate the adoption of quantum-secure blockchain solutions.

As the quantum threat looms on the horizon, the need to prepare cryptocurrency protocols and infrastructure for the quantum era becomes imperative. Blockchain developers and cryptocurrency enthusiasts alike are spearheading efforts to upgrade existing protocols and infrastructure to withstand quantum attacks. From migrating to quantum-resistant cryptographic primitives to implementing quantum-safe key management practices, these proactive measures aim to future-proof decentralized networks against the disruptive potential of quantum computing.

The quest for quantum security in blockchain technology represents a pivotal chapter in the ongoing evolution of digital trust and security. Through the convergence of post-quantum cryptography, quantum-resistant algorithms, and quantum key distribution, blockchain ecosystems can fortify their defenses against the looming threat of quantum computing. With collaborative efforts driving innovation and resilience, the future of blockchain remains bright, anchored in a quantum-secure foundation poised to withstand the tests of time and technology.

Bridging the Gap: Empowering Underserved Communities with Blockchain

In the vast tapestry of global finance, there exists a stark divide between the privileged and the marginalized. While traditional financial systems cater to the affluent, billions of individuals in developing regions find themselves excluded from formal banking services. However, amidst this disparity, blockchain technology emerges as a beacon of hope, offering transformative solutions to empower underserved communities and foster financial inclusion.

At the forefront of this movement are blockchain-based microfinance and peer-to-peer lending platforms, revolutionizing access to capital for those on the fringes of the financial system. By leveraging blockchain's decentralized architecture and smart contract capabilities, these platforms enable individuals to borrow, lend, and invest funds without the need for intermediaries. From small-scale entrepreneurs seeking microloans to rural farmers in need of agricultural financing, blockchain-powered microfinance initiatives provide a lifeline to those traditionally excluded from traditional banking services.

Education and awareness campaigns play a pivotal role in fostering cryptocurrency adoption and financial literacy in underprivileged areas. Through grassroots initiatives and community outreach programs, organizations educate individuals about the fundamentals of blockchain technology, cryptocurrencies, and decentralized finance. By empowering individuals with the knowledge and tools to navigate the digital economy, these campaigns pave the way for greater participation and inclusion in the global financial landscape.

In addition to providing access to financial services, blockchain technology offers innovative solutions to address the unique challenges faced by underserved communities. For instance, blockchain-based identity systems enable individuals in developing regions to establish verifiable digital identities, unlocking access to essential services such as healthcare, education, and social welfare. Moreover, blockchain-powered supply chain platforms empower small-scale producers to access global markets, bypassing traditional barriers and securing fair compensation for their goods.

Collaborative efforts between governments, NGOs, and private sector entities are essential to scale financial inclusion initiatives and maximize their impact. By fostering partnerships and leveraging local expertise, stakeholders can design tailored solutions that address the specific needs and challenges of underserved communities. From regulatory frameworks that support blockchain innovation to investment in infrastructure and capacity-building initiatives, concerted action is key to unlocking the full potential of blockchain technology in advancing financial inclusion.

Furthermore, the proliferation of mobile technology presents a unique opportunity to accelerate financial inclusion efforts in developing regions. With the widespread adoption of smartphones and mobile internet connectivity, blockchain-based financial services can reach remote communities previously underserved by traditional banking infrastructure. By harnessing the power of mobile applications and digital wallets, individuals can access a wide range of financial services, including payments, savings, and investments, from the palm of their hand.

As we strive towards a more inclusive and equitable global financial system, blockchain technology emerges as a powerful tool for driving positive change. By empowering underserved communities with access to capital, knowledge, and opportunity, blockchain-based initiatives have the potential to uplift millions out of poverty and catalyze sustainable economic development. Through collaborative efforts and innovative solutions, we can build a future where financial inclusion is not just a privilege but a fundamental human right for all.

Chapter Ten
Revolutionizing Healthcare with Blockchain Technology

In the realm of healthcare, where trust, security, and transparency are paramount, blockchain technology emerges as a disruptive force, poised to revolutionize the industry. From electronic health records (EHRs) to supply chain management and clinical trials, blockchain solutions offer transformative benefits that promise to enhance patient care, streamline operations, and safeguard sensitive data.

At the forefront of this transformation are electronic health records (EHRs) stored on the blockchain. Unlike traditional EHR systems siloed within individual healthcare providers, blockchain-based EHRs offer interoperability, allowing seamless sharing of patient data across disparate systems. Moreover, by encrypting health records and granting patients ownership and control over their data, blockchain technology enhances privacy and empowers individuals to actively participate in their healthcare journey.

Supply chain transparency is another area where blockchain technology shines in the healthcare sector. With counterfeit drugs and medical devices posing significant risks to patient safety, blockchain-based solutions offer unprecedented visibility and traceability throughout the supply chain. By recording the entire lifecycle of pharmaceuticals and medical devices on an immutable ledger, stakeholders can verify authenticity, track provenance, and mitigate the proliferation of counterfeit products.

In the realm of clinical trials and medical research, blockchain solutions hold promise for enhancing data integrity, transparency, and collaboration. By recording trial data on a tamper-proof blockchain ledger, researchers can ensure the integrity and immutability of research findings, bolstering trust and confidence in the scientific process. Moreover, blockchain-based platforms facilitate secure data sharing and collaboration among researchers, accelerating the pace of medical discovery and innovation.

Disease surveillance is another critical area where blockchain technology can make a profound impact. By leveraging decentralized networks and secure data sharing protocols, blockchain-based surveillance systems enable real-time monitoring of disease outbreaks, epidemiological trends, and public health emergencies. By enhancing data accuracy, timeliness, and interoperability, these systems empower healthcare authorities to implement targeted interventions and mitigate the spread of infectious diseases.

Collaboration and partnerships between stakeholders are essential to harnessing the full potential of blockchain technology in healthcare. From healthcare providers and pharmaceutical companies to technology firms and regulatory agencies, collective action is key to overcoming barriers and driving adoption. By fostering an ecosystem of innovation and collaboration, stakeholders can co-create blockchain solutions that address the unique challenges and opportunities in healthcare.

Moreover, regulatory frameworks must evolve to accommodate the unique characteristics of blockchain technology while ensuring patient privacy, data security, and regulatory compliance. By establishing clear guidelines and standards for blockchain implementation in healthcare, regulators can provide certainty and confidence to industry participants, fostering innovation while safeguarding patient interests.

Blockchain technology holds immense promise for transforming the healthcare industry, from improving patient care and safety to enhancing data integrity and transparency. By leveraging blockchain solutions for electronic health records, supply chain management, clinical trials, and disease surveillance, stakeholders can unlock new opportunities for innovation and collaboration. As we embark on this journey towards a blockchain-powered healthcare future, collaboration, innovation, and a commitment to patient-centricity will be essential to realizing the full potential of this transformative technology.

AI-Powered Cryptocurrency Trading and Risk Management

In the fast-paced world of cryptocurrency markets, where volatility reigns supreme, traditional trading strategies often fall short. However, amidst the chaos, artificial intelligence (AI) emerges as a game-changer, revolutionizing the way traders analyze data, execute trades, and manage risk. From algorithmic trading strategies to machine learning applications, AI-driven approaches offer unparalleled insights and capabilities that empower traders to navigate the complex landscape of digital assets with confidence.

Algorithmic trading strategies and high-frequency trading (HFT) have become cornerstones of the cryptocurrency market, enabling traders to capitalize on fleeting opportunities and execute trades at lightning speed. By leveraging advanced algorithms and automation, algorithmic traders seek to exploit inefficiencies in the market, executing trades based on predefined rules and parameters. Meanwhile, high-frequency traders harness the power of cutting-edge technology to execute a large volume of trades within fractions of a second, profiting from minute price discrepancies across exchanges.

Machine learning applications play a pivotal role in enhancing price prediction, sentiment analysis, and market forecasting in cryptocurrency trading. Through the analysis of vast amounts of historical data, machine learning algorithms can identify patterns, correlations, and trends that elude human traders. From predicting price movements to gauging market sentiment and identifying trading opportunities, machine learning models offer valuable insights that inform decision-making and drive profitability in cryptocurrency markets.

Risk management is paramount in cryptocurrency trading, where volatility and uncertainty abound. AI and data analytics empower traders to implement sophisticated risk management techniques that mitigate exposure and protect portfolios from adverse market conditions. By analyzing market data in real-time, AI-driven risk management systems can identify potential risks and execute preemptive measures such as stop-loss orders and portfolio rebalancing to minimize losses and preserve capital.

Moreover, AI-powered portfolio optimization techniques enable traders to construct diversified portfolios that maximize returns while minimizing risk. By leveraging advanced algorithms and optimization models, traders can identify optimal asset allocations based on risk tolerance, investment objectives, and market conditions. Furthermore, machine learning algorithms can adapt and evolve over time, continuously optimizing portfolio strategies in response to changing market dynamics and emerging trends.

As the cryptocurrency market continues to evolve, the role of AI in trading is poised to expand, driving innovation and reshaping the landscape of digital asset management. From algorithmic trading strategies and machine learning applications to risk management techniques and portfolio optimization, AI empowers traders with the tools and insights needed to thrive in the dynamic and competitive world of cryptocurrency trading. By harnessing the power of AI-driven approaches, traders can unlock new opportunities, mitigate risks, and achieve their financial goals in the ever-changing cryptocurrency market.

Conclusion

As we stand on the precipice of a new era in finance, it's essential to reflect on the remarkable evolution of cryptocurrency. From its humble beginnings as a fringe technology to its current status as a global phenomenon, cryptocurrency has traversed a tumultuous path filled with challenges, triumphs, and paradigm shifts. Yet, amidst the chaos and uncertainty, one thing remains clear: the transformative potential of cryptocurrency to revolutionize society and finance as we know it.

Embracing innovation and adaptation has been central to cryptocurrency's success in navigating a rapidly changing landscape. In the face of regulatory scrutiny, technological hurdles, and market volatility, cryptocurrency developers, entrepreneurs, and enthusiasts have demonstrated resilience and ingenuity, pushing the boundaries of what's possible and driving forward the adoption and acceptance of digital assets. Through constant innovation and adaptation, cryptocurrency has evolved from a niche curiosity to a mainstream asset class with the potential to reshape the global financial system.

The potential of cryptocurrency to transform society and finance is profound and far-reaching. Beyond its role as a digital currency, cryptocurrency represents a paradigm shift in the way we think about money, value, and trust. By decentralizing financial transactions and disintermediating traditional institutions, cryptocurrency empowers individuals with greater control over their finances, fostering financial inclusion, and economic empowerment for millions around the world.

Moreover, cryptocurrency has the potential to democratize access to financial services, particularly in underserved and marginalized communities. Through blockchain technology, individuals can access banking services, credit, and investment opportunities without the need for traditional intermediaries, leveling the playing field and providing a pathway to economic opportunity for those historically excluded from the formal financial system.

Furthermore, cryptocurrency's underlying technology, blockchain, holds promise for revolutionizing industries beyond finance, including supply chain management, healthcare, and governance. By enabling transparent, secure, and immutable record-keeping, blockchain technology enhances efficiency, accountability, and trust in a wide range of applications, paving the way for greater transparency, integrity, and innovation across various sectors.

As we look towards the future, it's clear that cryptocurrency's journey is far from over. With each passing day, new challenges and opportunities emerge, driving forward the evolution of digital assets and shaping the trajectory of finance and society. Yet, amidst the uncertainty and volatility, one thing remains certain: the transformative potential of cryptocurrency to empower individuals, foster innovation, and create a more inclusive and equitable world for all.

In conclusion, cryptocurrency's evolution is a testament to the power of innovation, adaptation, and resilience in the face of adversity. As we continue to navigate the ever-changing landscape of digital finance, it's imperative that we embrace the potential of cryptocurrency to transform society and finance for the better. By harnessing the power of innovation and collaboration, we can unlock new opportunities, overcome challenges, and build a future where cryptocurrency plays a central role in shaping a more equitable and prosperous world.

www.ingramcontent.com/pod-product-compliance
Lightning Source LLC
Chambersburg PA
CBHW070400230526
45471CB00006B/2655